MAKING
GARDEN
ORNAMENTS

MAKING
GARDEN
ORNAMENTS

Pretty and practical
accessories to make

Consultant editor: Simona Hill

First published in 2000 by
Lorenz Books

© Anness Publishing Limited 2000

Lorenz Books
is an imprint of
Anness Publishing Limited
Hermes House
88–89 Blackfriars Road
London SE1 8HA

Published in the USA by Lorenz Books,
Anness Publishing Inc., 27 West 20th Street,
New York, NY 10011; (800) 354-9657

This edition distributed in Canada by Raincoast Books,
8680 Cambie Street, Vancouver, British Columbia V6P 6M9

ISBN 0 7548 0461 5

A CIP catalogue record for this book is available from the British Library

Publisher: Joanna Lorenz
Project Editor: Simona Hill
Designer: Simon Wilder
Editorial Reader: Hayley Kerr
Production Controller: Claire Rae

Printed and bound in China

3 5 7 9 10 8 6 4

Contents

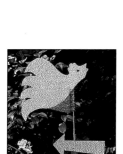

Introduction

A trellis arch made of willow graces a garden wall and is sturdy enough to support climbing plants.

A few well-chosen garden ornaments add instant impact to a garden. Grouped together in a visually pleasing way, they present a colourful and interesting focal point. Carefully placed, they can be used to direct the attention out towards the boundaries, to draw the eye to certain parts of the garden or to add interest to a dull and dark area. Ornaments can also direct how the garden is used and appreciated, such as a strategically-placed seat from which to take in a particularly pretty spot, or a birdbath to attract birds to the garden.

When you're designing a garden, it's natural to think first about the plants you are looking forward to growing in it, but it soon becomes obvious that the plants are only half the story. Like the walls and floors inside the home, the garden's basic structure defines the space and sets the tone of the garden. And, just like the rooms in your home, the way you decorate your outdoor living space – with colour, texture and ornament – plays a big part in creating your garden's unique personality, and in stamping your own style on your surroundings. Afterall, the garden is a part of your home, that just happens to be outside.

Colour in the garden need not come solely from the plants. Paint or woodstains in carefully chosen colours, used for planters,

* *A shell-encrusted terracotta pot makes a pleasing focal point and looks good planted with simple textural foliage.*

pots and containers, can make a dramatic setting for flowers and foliage. Adding colour has become much easier now that exterior paint ranges are no longer restricted to shades of green and brown but include fresh-looking blues, pinks and lilacs. For maximum impact, stick to a colour theme, and use shades that complement your planting scheme.

Pots of plants always look charming, especially if they are in a carefully arranged group. Pots and containers of all kinds make infinitely adaptable garden decorations. There is little to beat the earthy beauty of ordinary clay pots. They blend happily with their surroundings and complement virtually every plant. The colour of terracotta pots softens with age as salts naturally form on the surface. You can hasten this look by scrubbing them with garden lime mixed to a thick paste with a little water. As the water in the lime dries out, the terracotta will acquire a soft, white bloom.

Almost anything can be used to hold plants, as long as drainage holes can be drilled in the base. Try using old beer barrel halves, old chimney pots, buckets, agricultural baskets or wooden trugs. With a little imagination, shopping baskets, birdcages and lanterns can become hanging baskets; old olive oil cans in a row can become window-boxes.

For centuries, stone statues and fountains have provided focal points at the end of vistas or charming surprises in secluded spots. Classical figures are still popular as reproductions. Old

* *Keep track of your newly-planted seeds with large-scale row markers.*

states, aged by lichens, natural salts and the passage of time, are exquisite but prohibitively expensive. However, as with flower pots, the ageing process can be accelerated on modern stone copies by coating them with live yogurt. Beautiful as these statues are, there are alternatives that may be far more relevant to your garden and more personal to you. Metal and wire sculpture works very well outside, as does willow, woven into dynamic figures.

Even in the more dense urban areas, gardens can be havens for wildlife. Many plants attract beneficial insects such as butterflies and bees, and birds are the most welcome of garden visitors: they are fascinating to watch, lovely to listen to, and they earn their keep by eating garden pests such as snails and aphids. Even better than garden visitors are permanent residents: nesting boxes are rewarding to watch when they are occupied, and can also be decorative garden features all year round. Birds naturally choose sheltered spots, so take care to place your birdhouse in a safe place, facing away from the prevailing wind and rain.

Clay decorations applied to terracotta pots give them a unique personality.

❋ *Verdigris or rust-effect lends the serenity of age to new galvanized buckets.*

Using lighting in the garden expands the usable living area and creates a different outdoor mood. As well as its purely practical effects, it allows the best features of the garden to be highlighted, and brings the garden to life in a totally different way. Candles must surely be the most romantic outdoor lighting. The ordinary candles you use on the dining table can simply be taken outside, candelabra and all, for a candle-lit dinner.

But if the night is at all breezy, use lanterns or some other holders which protect the flames from the elements.

As well as lanterns, you could try Victorian nightlights, which are tumbler-like glass containers hung on wires, huge glass hanging lanterns, candles in garden pots or galvanized buckets which – once they burn down below the rim – are protected from the wind. You need to bear in mind when using outdoor candles and flares that the wind does fan the flames, so it is important always to position them well away from any foliage or furniture and never leave them unattended.

Brightly-coloured, flower-shaped candleholders are made of foil and decorate the garden at evening time.

Like the pictures on your walls and the porcelain on your mantelpiece, garden ornaments are the finishing touches in the overall design. So when your garden is looking beautiful and you really want to draw attention to its design and its planting, some well-judged artefacts will draw the eye.

While ready-made garden ornaments provide an instant solution, it is so much more satisfying to make your own. Whatever your interest, here is a fun and inspirational selection of ornaments to decorate floors and walls, to add interest in the vegetable patch or to brighten up a dull corner of the patio. None of these projects require special skills or training. Most use materials that are cheap to buy and are readily available in the high street. Making your own ornaments is tremendous fun, and a great way to stamp a unique and individual style on a special plot of land.

Encourage birds to visit your garden by introducing this beaten copper birdbath.

Pots and Planters

Pots and containers are indispensable for adding colour and interest to the garden. By planting up portable pots you can put the colour where you want it. All containers, however simple, add architectural form to the garden.

Transforming an ordinary flower pot into something special really doesn't have to be difficult. There are so many media to choose from. Stencilled designs look stylish and distinctive, and even plain colours can be striking: a pot painted in clear Mediterranean blue and planted with scarlet pelargoniums will enliven the dullest corner of the garden or patio. Choose paint colours that will enhance your plants and look good within your garden's colour scheme. Terracotta is porous and will absorb a lot of paint, so you may need several coats, depending on the colour you are using.

An easy option is to glue decorations on to your pots – ceramic chips (tiles), perhaps, to make a mosaic, or shells arranged in a simple textural pattern. If you break a favourite plate or dish, using it to decorate a pot is a delightful way to continue to enjoy its colour and pattern.

✳ Mosaic Flower Pot ✳

As only part of the pot is covered with mosaic (tesserae), you will need to start with a glazed, high-fired terracotta pot; this is especially important if the pot is to be left outside during the winter.

You will need

flower pot

chalk or wax crayon

selection of china

tile nippers

flexible knife

cement-based tile adhesive

powdered waterproof tile grout

mixing container

cement dye

nailbrush

soft cloth

1 Draw a simple design on the pot, using chalk or a wax crayon. Accurately cut appropriate shapes from the china using tile nippers.

2 With the knife, apply some tile adhesive to the pot and stick on the tesserae. Work on a small area at a time so that you can follow the design.

3 Fill in the larger background areas of plain colour. When complete, leave the pot to dry for 24 hours. Mix powdered grout with water and a little cement dye.

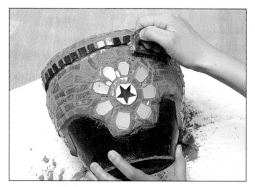

4 Spread the grout over the mosaic. Fill all the spaces. Allow to dry. Brush off any excess grout with a nailbrush. Dry for 48 hours, then polish with a soft cloth.

✳ Gilded Urn ✳

Bring a flash of gold to the garden with this striking urn, which started life as a humble plastic planter. It is gilded with inexpensive Dutch metal leaf and given an antique patina with a simple paint technique.

You will need

plastic plant urn

sandpaper

red oxide spray primer

water-based size

paintbrushes

gold Dutch metal leaf

burnishing brush or soft cloth

wire (steel) wool

methylated spirits (turpentine)

amber shellac varnish

acrylic paints in pale blue and grey

paint-mixing tray

1 Sand the surface of the urn to provide a key for the paint to adhere to. Spray with red oxide spray primer and leave to dry.

2 Paint on a thin, even coat of water-based size over the surface and leave for 20–30 minutes, until it becomes clear and tacky.

3 Carefully lay the gold Dutch metal leaf on to the surface to cover the whole area. Burnish with a burnishing brush or soft cloth to bring up the lustre.

4 Dip some wire (steel) wool into a little methylated spirit (turpentine) and rub the raised areas of the urn to distress the surface, rubbing lightly.

5 Seal with a thin, even coat of amber shellac varnish and leave to dry for 45 minutes to one hour.

6 Mix blue and grey acrylic paint with a little water. Paint the urn and leave for 5 minutes. Rub off most of the paint using a cloth, allowing just a little to remain in the areas of detail. Dampen the cloth if the paint has set too much. Leave to dry.

Decorated Terracotta Flower Pots

As terracotta pots age they acquire a beautiful patina of moss, algae and crystallized minerals, but brand new machine-made pots can also be given a unique personality with applied clay decorations.

You will need

tracing paper

pencil

stiff card (card stock)

craft knife

cutting mat

modelling clay

rolling pin

terracotta pots

masking tape

wood glue

contour paste for ceramics

talcum powder

cake decorating (cookie) cutters

tape measure

scrap paper

acrylic or emulsion (latex) paints

paintbrushes

matt acrylic varnish

1 Trace each "wax seal" design on to card (card stock). Cut out a round seal and the motif. Flatten a ball of clay. Press the template into it to make an indent.

2 If the pot you are decorating is round, use tape to attach the motif to the pot while the clay dries. Remove the tape and stick the motif to the pot using wood glue.

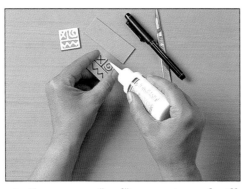

3 For a square "seal", cut a piece of stiff card to shape and decorate with contour paste in a simple design. Allow to dry thoroughly.

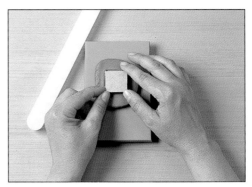

4 Roll out a small amount of clay. Dust the surface lightly with talcum powder. Press the seal into the clay, then remove it carefully.

5 Place the motif on the cutting mat and work around it with a sharp knife. Use tape to attach the motif to the pot while the clay dries. Remove the tape and stick the motif to the pot using wood glue.

6 For the ribbon bow, use a cutter or draw a bow design freehand. Roll out some clay 3mm/¹/₈in thick. Press the cutter firmly into the clay, then remove the excess. Neaten any rough edges.

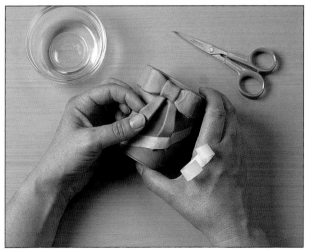

7 Fold the pieces into a bow shape and attach the "knot" piece by folding it over the front of the bow. You may need to practise several freehand bow designs before achieving a perfect bow.

8 Moisten the clay to stick the pieces together, then arrange the bow on the pot. Lift the ribbon ends slightly. Secure to the pot with masking tape until the bow is dry enough to glue in place.

Continued over ➤

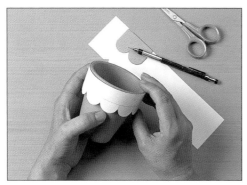

9 For the scalloped cuff, measure the circumference of the top of the pot, then draw the cuff on paper to fit the pot.

10 Roll out a length of clay 3mm/¹⁄₈in thick. Place the template on top and cut out with the knife. Neaten any rough edges. Place the cuff around the rim of the pot. Moisten the edges to join them neatly. Work some clay over the seam with your fingers to tidy it up and secure with masking tape. Allow the pots to dry upside down.

11 If you wish, paint the pots with acrylic or emulsion (latex) paints. Protect with several coats of varnish.

✳ *Metallic-effect Buckets* ✳

There is something irresistible about the luminous, blue-green tones of verdigris. It is a colour that always complements plants. Use the same technique to produce a rusted effect.

You will need

galvanized buckets

medium-grade sandpaper

metal primer

paintbrushes

acrylic paints in gold, white, aqua and rust

amber shellac

natural sponge

polyurethane varnish

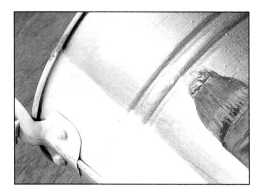

1 Sand the buckets, then prime with metal primer and allow to dry. Give each bucket a coat of gold paint and leave to dry for 2–3 hours.

2 Add a coat of shellac. Allow to dry. For verdigris, mix white and aqua paint and dilute to a watery consistency. For the rust, mix white with rust and dilute.

✳ *Using the same technique and different colourways, this plastic planter has been made to resemble a lead chimney.*

3 Sponge the thinned paint over the shellac, allowing the gold base coat to show through in places. Leave to dry for 1–2 hours. Apply a coat of varnish.

✳ Shell Pots ✳

*Shell-encrusted flower pots are so decorative in themselves that it's best
to plant them with simple foliage. White tile cement has been used for
this dramatic black and white design, which shimmers with seed beads.*

You will need

selection of shells

paper towels

terracotta pot

tile cement

putty knife or
spreader

seed beads

1 If the shells need cleaning, scrub them
thoroughly and drain on paper towels.
Clean the pot, then spread tile cement
thickly over a section of the side.

2 Work out your design on paper first,
then arrange the shells in the cement,
aiming for good contrasts of shape and
colour, and embedding them deeply.

3 If the cement is too obtrusive for your
taste, sprinkle on seed beads or
ground-up shells while the surface is still
sticky. Shake off any excess.

4 It is easier to apply the shells to the
pot in sections. You can let the pot
rest on its side as the completed section
dries before starting on the next.

Hanging Ornaments

The ideal garden is a feast for all the senses, and its gentle outdoor sounds are harmonious and soothing. The murmur of bees, the rustle of leaves in the breeze and the choruses of small birds conjure up a picture of a perfect summer day. Birds will flock to your garden if you provide food on a birdtable in the winter and a bird-bath in the summer. Both can be beautiful and decorative additions to your garden. Hang them in a safe place, out of reach of neighbourhood cats, and remember that if you feed garden birds in winter you must do so regularly, as they will come to depend on you.

Wind chimes will tinkle prettily as they move in the breeze, especially if you make them from natural materials such as bamboo or shells. Hang a mobile or some wind chimes in the branches of a favourite tree: each time it catches your eye you'll notice afresh the tree's delicate foliage and the dappled shadows it casts. Shiny materials used for mobiles will add their reflections to the interplay of light, and in the evening, candles in hanging lanterns and chandeliers will create some garden magic.

✽ *Wind Chimes* ✽

A walk on the beach or in the woods to gather weathered driftwood and twigs, and a forage in the potting shed, will provide you with all the materials you need to make these rustic wind chimes.

You will need

110cm/44in galvanized wire

wire cutters

drill

four twigs, different sizes, the largest 30cm/12in long

three corks

two vine-eyes (metal rings)

5cm/2in old terracotta pots

bells

1 Cut one 50cm/20in and two 30cm/12in lengths of wire. Drill a hole through the centre of each cork.

2 Make a hanging loop at one end of the longer piece of wire. Just beneath the loop, twist the wire around the centre of the longest twig and thread on a cork.

3 Add the next twig, either twisting the wire around it as before, or drilling a hole and threading it on. Add a cork, a third twig and the third cork.

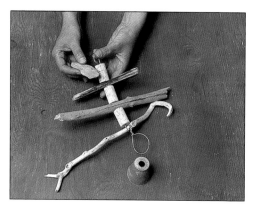

4 Make a hook in the end of the wire, trimming it if necessary. Drill a hole through one end of the final twig and thread it on to the hook.

5 Thread a vine-eye (metal ring) on to each of the shorter lengths of wire. Bend over 2.5cm/1in of wire so it lies flat against the vine-eye. Wrap the long end of the wire around the vine-eye in a spiral.

6 Thread each wired vine-eye through the drainage hole in one of the terracotta pots. Hang up the wind chimes and attach the bells by twisting their wires around the longest twig. Adjust their positions if necessary so that the chimes balance. Hang in place.

✻ Copper Birdbath ✻

You will have endless pleasure watching the birds preening and cleaning in this beautiful yet eminently practical beaten copper birdbath.

1 Using a chinagraph pencil (china marker) and a piece of string looped around a suction cap, accurately mark a 45cm/18in circle on the copper sheet.

2 Wearing protective gloves, cut out the circle with tin snips. Smooth the sharp edge of the tin using a metal file.

3 Place the circle on a blanket and hammer it lightly from the centre. Spread the dips out to the rim. Repeat, until you have the required shape.

4 To make the perch, loop 1m/39in copper wire and hold the ends in a vice. Fasten a cup hook into the chuck of a drill. Put the hook through the loop and run the drill at slow speed to twist the wire. Drill three holes, equally spaced, around the rim of the bath.

5 Divide the remaining wire into three equal lengths and knot one end of each. Thread through the holes from beneath. Slip the twisted wire over two straight wires to form a perch. Bend the tops of the hanging wires into a loop.

Wire and Feather Hanging *

This decorative hanging is made from garden wire, twigs picked up in the garden and a few feathers. When it is hanging in a tree, the slightest breeze will set the feathers in motion and draw the eye.

You will need

90cm/36in thick plastic-coated garden wire

wire cutters

pliers

reel of thin plastic-coated garden wire

pencil

two twigs, about 18cm/7in long

three feathers

black thread

1 Cut the thick wire in half and use pliers to bend both pieces into smooth, S-shapes. Make the shapes match.

2 Using the thin wire, join the two S-shapes securely together so that the small "curls" are positioned back to back.

3 Make the decorative spiral by twisting a length of thin wire around the seam, then winding it around a pencil. Remove the pencil and trim the spiral to about 10cm/4in.

4 Wire the twigs into a V-shape using thin wire. Fasten to the wire structure. Tie the feathers together and suspend them below the decoration. Tie thread to the top for hanging.

※ This filigree heart, made from
ordinary garden wire, makes a pretty,
decorative hanging feature. It is made of
several small hearts, each bent into shape
with household pliers. The hearts are
bound together with fine wire into one
heart shape.

❋ Mosaic Hearts ❋

Most gardens are a source of treasure, however modest. As you turn the soil, you are bound to uncover broken and weathered pieces of china and glass: save them to make decorative small mosaics.

You will need

heart-shaped cookie cutter

petroleum jelly

green garden wire

scissors

stiff card (card stock)

cement-based tile adhesive

weathered pieces of glass

1 Coat the inside edge of the cookie cutter with petroleum jelly to make removing the finished mosaic easier.

2 To make a hanging loop, cut a short length of green garden wire and bend it into a loop.

3 Position the loop at the top of the heart with the ends of the wire under the edge of the mould and bent up inside it. This will ensure the sharp ends are completely covered by the tile cement.

4 Place the mould on the card (card stock) and half fill it with tile cement. Carefully smooth the surface of the cement with wet fingers.

5 Arrange the pieces of glass on the surface of the cement. If you need to reposition a piece, wash off any cement before replacing it.

6 Leave the mosaic to dry for at least 24 hours. When the cement feels solid to the touch, gently remove the mosaic from the mould.

✳ Garden Chandelier ✳

*Decorate your garden for the festive season with this beautiful candle
ring hung with dried oranges and starfish dusted with gold. It looks
perfect hanging from a bare branch in a frosty winter garden.*

You will need

dried oranges

knife

screwdriver

stub (floral) wires

glue gun

moss

small plastic starfish

gold spray paint

rope

ready-made hop-
vine or twig ring

4 florist's candle
holders

4 candles

1 Cut each orange in half and make a
hole in each half with a screwdriver.
Push the two ends of a bent stub (floral)
wire through the hole, making a loop.

2 Bend the ends of the wire up inside
the orange to hold the loop securely.
Coat the inside of the orange with glue.
Push moss into the space to fill it.

3 Glue starfish on to the moss and
around the orange. Add a few more to
the top and bottom of the oranges.

4 Bend the top and bottom of a stub
wire into hooks, hang the decoration
on one end and spray it lightly with gold.
Make all the decorations in the same way.

5 Tie ropes firmly to the ring in four
places, so that the chandelier hangs
horizontally. Push a handful of moss into
the ring between two of the ropes.

6 Make a hole in the centre, glue it and
insert a candle holder. Put a candle
into the holder to make sure it is straight.
Repeat on the other three sides.

Functional Decorations

Some of the most telling decorative effects in the garden stem from artefacts that combine beauty with a purpose. An old garden fork, its handle polished with use, a galvanized watering can, turned soft grey with time, or a wheelbarrow, pitted with wear, all have attractive forms that can give structure to the garden. Leave your well-used garden tools where they were last used and they will reward you with their decorative appeal.

Ordinary gardening tasks become far more pleasurable when your tools and accessories are beautiful as well as useful. Plant supports and seed-bed row markers are garden essentials, but that doesn't mean they can't be decorative too. If you want to attract birds to your garden, there's no reason why a functional, safe birdhouse shouldn't also be prettily decorated – the birds won't mind.

Weathervanes may no longer be essential, but they are not fripperies and are still able to serve a purpose. They exude a functional quality that is honest and pleasing, as well as making an effective focal point in a formal garden.

❋ Daisy Birdhouse ❋

Many small birds make rewarding and fascinating tenants in the garden. Substitute any flowers of your choice for these bright daisies, to produce customized garden chic for the resident birds.

You will need

6mm/¼in medium density fibreboard (MDF) or exterior-grade plywood

protective face mask

pencil

ruler

coping saw

PVA (white) glue

hammer

panel pins (brads)

bench vice

drill

emulsion (latex) paint in white, yellow, green and blue

medium and fine paintbrushes

glue gun

exterior-grade varnish

1 Mark out the pieces for the basic house in MDF or plywood, following the template. Cut out and assemble using PVA (white) glue and panel pins (brads).

2 Cut out the leaf and petals. Using a drill and coping saw, cut out the centre hole of the front motif to match the flower centre. Paint the pieces and leave to dry.

3 Paint the house blue. When dry, embellish with painted "grass". Paint the entrance yellow, but leave the interior unpainted for the sake of the birds' health.

4 Glue the shapes to the box. Position the shapes to form a "daisy chain" across the roof, and add some petals on the sides. Protect with layers of varnish.

❋ Willow Heart ❋

Let your plants twine around this heart-shaped support: the centre of the motif can be filled with a weave of any material. For the central stick, choose something with attractive bark, such as hazel or cherry.

You will need

tape measure

two 1.5m/5ft brown willow rods

secateurs (pruning shears)

string

six 1.2m/4ft brown willow rods

bodkin

45cm/18in straight hedgerow stick

90cm/3ft slender brown willow rod

trailing vine stems

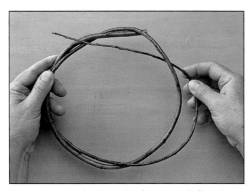

1 Twist the butt end of a 1.5m/5ft willow rod into a 18cm/7in hoop. Wrap the tip end round the hoop. Add the second rod, wrapping in the other direction.

2 Trim all the ends. Tie the butt ends of the 1.2m/4ft rods together and clamp them. Make a three-strand plait (braid) 15cm/6in long, using doubled rods.

3 Divide the rods of the plait into two sets of three, taking one rod from each group of two. Place the hoop between the two groups.

4 Twist the two groups over each other twice to make a rope. Enclose the opposite side of the hoop and divide the rods into two groups again.

5 Bring the ends of the groups around into a heart shape, twisting them as you go. Catch in the sides of the hoop as you reach it. Use a bodkin to thread the ends into the plait.

6 Push the end of the stick into the top of the heart, then remove the string tie and bind the base of the plait to the stick with a slender willow rod. Fill in the heart with a weave of trailing material.

Decorative Plant Support

Broom handles form the centre of this ingenious design, which makes an ideal support for annual climbers such as sweet peas. At the end of the season it can be folded away until it is needed again.

You will need

three wooden knobs, 4cm/1½in in diameter

three broom handles

PVA (white) glue

matt woodwash or emulsion (latex) paint

paintbrush

drill

sisal rope

tape measure

craft knife

1 Glue a wooden knob to the end of each broom handle using PVA (white) glue. Leave to dry for a few hours, preferably overnight.

2 Paint the supports with two coats of matt woodwash or emulsion (latex) paint, allowing them to dry thoroughly between coats.

3 Drill a hole through each support, about 30cm/12in from the top, large enough to take the sisal rope. Cut a 40cm/16in length of rope and thread it through the holes. Tie the rope in a reef knot (that is, left over right and then right over left), so that the three supports form a tripod.

4 Tie a knot about 7.5cm/3in from each end of the rope to prevent it unravelling and fray the ends for a decorative effect.

✳ Weathervane ✳

You don't need metal-working skills to make this cheerful weathervane.
The shapes are cut out of rigid plastic (acrylic) sheet covered with roof
flashing, which is then given a hammered texture.

You will need

paper

scissors

marker pen

rigid plastic (acrylic)
sheet

coping saw

scrap wood

drill

craft knife

small paint roller

galvanized wire

self-adhesive roof-
flashing

straight edge

hacksaw

metal file

brass screw

screwdriver

broom handle

newspaper

hammer

blue glass paint

paintbrush

1 Enlarge the template and draw the arrow. Cut out paper patterns. Mark the shapes on the plastic and cut out. Drill a row of small holes and an eye.

2 Cut the central plastic tube from a paint roller and use wire to attach it to the rooster. Cut strips of roof-flashing to cover the plastic shapes. Trim the edges.

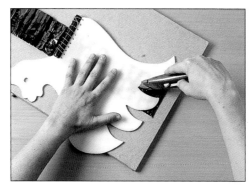

3 Apply the strips to both sides of the rooster and arrow. Butt the long edges together. Trim around the shape. Wrap the lower strips around the roller.

4 Cut out the eye and drill a small hole for the screw. Using a hacksaw, cut off the bent section of the paint roller handle. File the sawn edges smooth.

5 Screw the arrow to the plastic roller handle. Fit the roller handle to the broom handle to make a mount for the weathervane.

6 Using a small hammer, tap gently and evenly all over both sides of the cockerel to give it texture. Colour the area marked on the template using blue glass paint. Mount the plastic roller tube on the metal rod.

Garden Candleholders

Plant an instant border of dazzling flower-shaped candleholders in bright metallic colours. As they are made from foil dishes (pans) and garden stakes, you can produce a large number for maximum impact.

You will need

deep-sided foil pie dishes (pans)

permanent marker

scissors

glass paints

paintbrush

small foil pie dishes (pans)

coloured foil (optional)

epoxy resin glue

tealights with metal cases

flat-headed 2.5cm/1in nails

green garden stakes

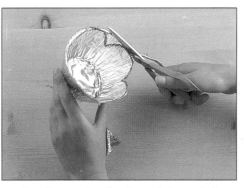

1 On the inside of a deep foil pie dish (pan) draw the outlines of six rounded petals. Cut out. Paint the flower, inside and out, with a bright colour. Leave to dry.

2 Cover a small pie dish with brightly coloured foil, if available, or paint it in a colour that will contrast with one you have used for the flower petals.

3 Glue the metal case from a tealight into the small dish, then place the dish inside the flower and push a nail through the centre of all three layers.

4 Push the point of the nail into the end of a stake. Add glue to the joint to hold it firmly together. When dry, put the tealight in the centre of the flower.

✳ Row Markers ✳

In spring, when seeds are germinating under the soil, there is a risk of losing track of what you have planted. While ordinary labels may get lost, these large-scale row markers certainly won't be misplaced.

You will need

wooden broom handles

ruler

saw

fine-grade sandpaper

wooden knobs, 4cm/1½in in diameter

PVA (white) glue

matt woodwash or emulsion (latex) paint

paintbrush

metal plant labels

gold permanent marker

garden string

drill (optional)

1 Cut a 70cm/28in length of broom handle. Sand the sawn edge and attach a wooden knob using PVA (white) glue. Leave to dry overnight.

2 Paint the marker with matt woodwash or emulsion (latex) paint. Brush a coat of paint on to a metal label. Leave to dry. Rub down lightly to give a distressed look.

3 Outline the label with gold pen and attach it to the marker by tying string around the knob, or drill a hole just below the knob and thread the string through.

✳ *Make row markers into a special feature in your garden plot.*

Walls and Floors

Walls give you the opportunity to add a vertical dimension to your planting, as they can support a host of climbers and wall shrubs. But even when your walls are well clothed, one or two thoughtfully placed ornaments give them style and interest. Wall-hung pots, sconces and items of statuary can all be used to enliven garden walls. As long as they are weatherproof, birdcages, birdfeeders, shells, lanterns, and willow or wire wreaths will also make good outdoor decorations. Ceramic tiled panels, mosaics, old enamel advertisements or painted wood panels all make excellent outdoor pictures.

Pebbles are a mosaic material with a centuries-old tradition. Their natural colours and smooth forms can be used to make exquisite textural floor panels or even complete garden floors. Simple geometric shapes are traditional, though in the hands of an artist, they can become elaborate, figurative works of art. A beautiful group of large pebbles, simply laid on the patio, makes a stunning decoration, or you could arrange them as part of a water feature, with the water bubbling gently through them.

House Number Plaque

The rising sun, a popular Art Deco motif, has been incorporated into the design of this plaque. It is decorated using a simple form of chasing, an ancient metalwork technique.

You will need

sheet of 30 gauge/0.01in tin plate

marker

ruler

protective gloves

tin snips

90° and 45° wooden blocks

bench vice

rubber mallet

file

graph paper

pencil

masking tape

chipboard

panel pins (brads)

centre punch

wire (steel) wool

clear polyurethane varnish

paintbrush

1 Draw a rectangle on a sheet of tin. Draw a 1cm/¹⁄₂in border inside the rectangle and mark diagonal lines across each corner. Cut out the plaque.

2 Clamp the 90° wood block in a vice. Align the inner edge of the border with the block edge. With a hammer, tap along the plaque edge to turn it over 90°.

3 Turn the plaque over. Put the 45° block in the turned edge. Tap the edge over it, remove the block and hammer the edge flat. Repeat on each side. File the corners.

4 Draw your pattern on a piece of graph paper and tape it to the front of the plaque. Secure the plaque to a piece of chipboard with panel pins (brads).

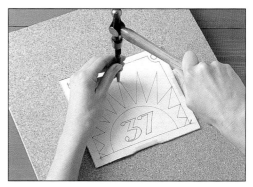

5 Place the punch on a line and tap it with a hammer to make an indent. Move the punch 3mm/¹⁄₈in and make the next mark. Punch along all the lines.

6 Remove the pattern, then punch the surface around the sunburst and inside the numbers. Scour the surface with wire (steel) wool and seal with varnish.

❋ *Trellis Fan Arch* ❋

This elegant willow trellis is easy to make. Held together with wire and nails, it is sturdy enough to support climbing plants, and makes a strong statement standing against a wall.

You will need

long, brown unstripped willow stems

garden wire

wire cutters

pruning saw

drill

hammer

small nails

raffia

scissors

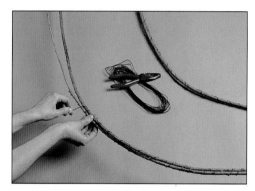

1 Bind two pairs of willow stems with wire. Bend to form two arches, the outer arch 168cm/66in high and the inner one 25cm/10in smaller.

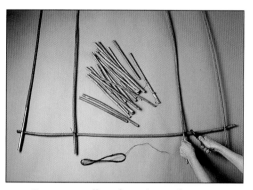

2 Cut two willow lengths to fit across the base of the arches. Bind the frame together with wire. Cut about 50 willow sticks 36cm/14in long.

3 Drill a hole 5cm/2in from each end of each stick. Space the sticks evenly around the arch in a radiating pattern and nail them in place.

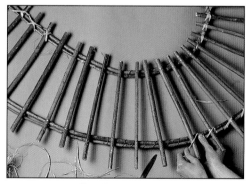

4 Using raffia, bind the sticks to the arch in one direction, then work back in the opposite direction to give a cross-stitch effect.

✳ Mosaic Slabs ✳

These large-scale pebble mosaics are very hard-wearing and can be repeated to lay as part of a path or patio. Using smaller frames, you can also create little pebble pictures to set in a floor or wall.

You will need

selection of pebbles

large sheet of paper

Four 38cm/15in-lengths of 5 x 2.5cm/2 x 1-in wood

hammer

nails

plastic (acrylic) sheet

protective gloves

cement

large bucket

1 Arrange the design first on a piece of paper the same size as the finished slab. Nail together the four pieces of wood to make a square frame.

2 Cover the work surface with a plastic (acrylic) sheet and put the frame in the centre. Wearing gloves, mix the cement. Fill the frame almost to the top.

3 Press the cement down into the corners, and smooth the surface. Transfer the pebbles to the cement, pressing each in place. Leave to set.

4 Free the slab by banging the edge of the frame firmly on a hard surface. Repeat the process to make as many slabs as you need.

❋ Painted Pebbles *❋*

For garden decoration, arrange a group of painted pebbles on a low wall or near a seat so that the subtle markings, textures and colours can be appreciated at close quarters.

You will need

selection of pebbles

rubber (latex) gloves

pencil

casein-based emulsion (latex) paint in black, white and ochre

fine paintbrushes

paint-mixing container

matt spray varnish

1 Wear gloves to handle the pebbles, as the grease from your fingers may affect them. Draw your design in pencil, then go over the lines in black paint.

2 Mix black and white paint to make different shades of grey. Use these to highlight areas of the design with a fine paintbrush.

3 Paint a random design on darker-coloured pebbles in white emulsion (latex) paint.

4 Instead of highlights, add depth using pale grey and ochre. Finally, add some details in black, using a very fine brush. Spray the pebbles with matt varnish.

❋ *Bacchus Garden Plaque* ❋

Set a convivial tone for summer parties in the garden by hanging this terracotta relief on the wall, so that the genial god of wine can gaze out from his leafy surroundings and smile benignly on the proceedings.

You will need

pencil

tracing paper

scissors

5mm/¼in rolling guides

rolling pin

modelling clay

sharp knife

hatpin or tapestry needle

modelling tools

5cm/2in strong wire

wire cutters

acrylic craft paints in red oxide and cream

paintbrushes

spray matt varnish

1 Enlarge the template, trace the outline and details and cut out. Roll out a slab of clay 5mm/¼in thick. Place the tracing on the clay and cut around the design.

2 Use a hatpin or needle to transfer the details on to the clay, by pricking along each line. Peel off the paper and smooth the edges with a modelling tool.

3 Draw in the features with a pointed modelling tool, using the pin-pricks as a guide. Press on small coils of clay for the hair.

4 Roll out the remaining clay to 5mm/¼in thick. Transfer the leaf shapes from the tracing. Fix them into place and mark the veins with a modelling tool.

Continued over ➤

5 Use small balls of clay for the grapes and coils for the beard.

6 Fix a loop of wire into the back to make a hanger, then leave the plaque to dry completely.

7 Mix red oxide and cream paint to make terracotta, and paint the plaque.

8 For a more weathered, textured effect, apply a second coat with a dry brush to give a stippled effect. Add highlights with a little cream paint, stippled on with a dry brush. Finish with several coats of matt varnish.

✳ Templates ✳

Enlarge the templates on a photocopier to the desired size.

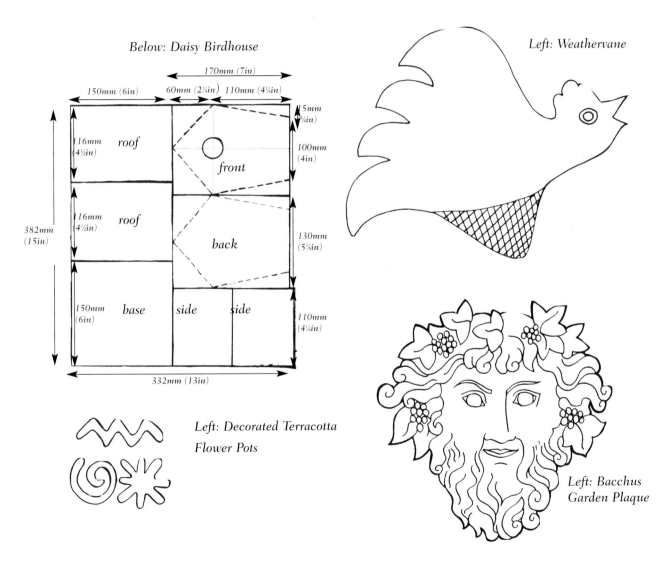

Below: Daisy Birdhouse

170mm (7in)

150mm (6in) 60mm (2¼in) 110mm (4¼in)

15mm (⅝in)

16mm (4½in)   roof

100mm (4in)

front

16mm (4½in)   roof

back

130mm (5⅛in)

382mm (15in)

150mm (6in)   base   side   side

110mm (4¼in)

332mm (13in)

Left: Weathervane

Left: Decorated Terracotta Flower Pots

Left: Bacchus Garden Plaque

✳ Index ✳

Acknowledgements

The publishers would like to thank the following contributors:
Helen Baird, Penny Boylan, Pattie Brown,
Andrew Newton Cox, Stephanie Donaldson, Marion Elliot,
Lucinda Ganderton, Andrew Gillmore, Mary Magurie,
Terence Moore, Deborah Schneebeli Morrell, Cleo Mussi,
Polly Pollock, Helen Smythe, Liz Wagstaff, and
Wendy Wilbrahams.

Thanks also to the following photographers:

Simon McBride, Rodney Forte, Michelle Garrett, Tim Imrie,
David Parmiter, Debbie Patterson, Peter Williams.